LEOPARD

MW01119433

FOR BEGINNERS

Gecko Seasonal Care, Myths, Safety Tips, Vet Care, Enrichment, Handling, Temperature, Feeding, Disease Prevention, Hydration, Breeding, Substrate, and Health Guide

Ethan Harry

Table of Contents

CHAPTER ONE

INTRODUCTION TO LEOPARD GECKOS

Leopard geckos are charming little reptiles that have become favorites among pet owners and reptile lovers worldwide. Their unique appearance, with bright colors and distinctive spots, makes them stand out from other lizards. These geckos are not just visually appealing; they are also known for their calm and gentle nature, which makes them an excellent choice for both beginners and experienced reptile keepers.

Leopard geckos are native to the dry, rocky regions of Afghanistan, Pakistan, India, and Iran. In the wild, they are used to a harsh environment with extreme temperatures, so they have developed some fascinating adaptations. For instance, they store fat in their tails, which helps them survive when food is scarce. Their skin, covered in tiny, bumpy scales, not only gives them their unique look but also helps protect them from the rough terrain they inhabit.

One of the most appealing aspects of leopard geckos as pets is their manageable size. They usually grow to about 8 to 10 inches long, making them easy to handle and care for. Their small size also means they don't need a lot of space, which is perfect for people who may not have a lot of room at home.

Leopard geckos are also relatively low-maintenance compared to some other reptiles. They don't require special lighting, like UVB lights, which are essential for many other lizard species. A simple heating pad or lamp to create a warm spot in their enclosure is usually enough to keep them comfortable. They are also easy to feed, as they primarily eat insects like crickets and mealworms, which are readily available at pet stores.

Another reason leopard geckos are so popular is their friendly and docile temperament. They are generally easy to handle and rarely bite, which makes them ideal for people who are new to keeping reptiles. With regular, gentle handling, leopard geckos can become quite tame and even seem to enjoy being held.

Understanding The Leopard Gecko

Leopard geckos (Eublepharis macularius) are small lizards that belong to the gecko family. They come from warm regions around the world and are popular pets because of their unique look and easygoing nature. Leopard geckos stand out from other geckos due to their appearance and habits. They have a sturdy body, short legs, and a broad head. Their skin is the most noticeable feature, with a pattern of yellow, orange, and black or brown spots, which looks similar to a leopard's coat—hence the name "leopard gecko."

One interesting thing about leopard geckos is that, unlike many other geckos, they have movable eyelids. This gives them a distinctive, almost expressive appearance, making them seem quite charming. Another difference is that they don't have the sticky toe pads that many other geckos use to climb smooth surfaces. So, you won't see them climbing the walls of their tank.

Instead, leopard geckos are ground-dwellers, perfectly suited to living on the ground rather than climbing.

Leopard geckos are crepuscular, which means they are most active during dawn and dusk. These are the times when they come out of their hiding spots to search for food. This behavior makes them easier to care for as pets since they don't need strong lighting that mimics the bright midday sun. A simple lighting setup that provides a natural day and night cycle is usually sufficient.

In terms of care, leopard geckos are relatively low-maintenance. They don't need a large or complicated habitat, and their diet is simple, consisting mainly of insects like crickets and mealworms. They also don't require the high humidity that some other reptiles need, which makes them an ideal choice for beginners. However, they do need a warm environment to thrive, so providing a heat source in their enclosure is important.

History And Natural Habitat

Leopard geckos are a popular choice among reptile enthusiasts, but their history as pets is fairly recent. Originally from South Asia, these geckos are native to countries like Afghanistan, Pakistan, India, and Iran. For centuries, local people in these regions have been familiar with leopard geckos, but it wasn't until the late 20th century that they began to gain popularity as pets in other parts of the world.

In the wild, leopard geckos live in rocky deserts and dry grasslands. These environments are challenging, with very hot days, cold nights, and limited water. To survive in such harsh conditions, leopard geckos have developed some fascinating adaptations. One of their most notable features is their ability to store fat in their tails. This fat reserve acts as an energy and hydration source when food and water are scarce, helping them survive during tough times.

Understanding the natural habitat of leopard geckos is important for anyone who wants to keep them as pets. By knowing where they come from, keepers can create an environment that closely mimics their natural surroundings. For example, providing a warm, dry enclosure with hiding spots and a substrate that allows for burrowing can help ensure that leopard geckos thrive in captivity. The temperature and humidity levels in their enclosure should reflect the conditions they would experience in the wild to keep them healthy and comfortable.

Leopard geckos have a long history of living alongside humans in their native regions. In some cultures, they are considered good luck charms, and their appetite for insects makes them natural pest controllers. Their calm nature and relatively simple care requirements have made them a favorite among reptile lovers around the world. Today, they are one of the most commonly kept and bred reptiles in the pet industry.

CHAPTER TWO

CHOOSING YOUR LEOPARD GECKO

Selecting A Healthy Gecko

When choosing a leopard gecko as a pet, it's important to pick one that is healthy. A healthy gecko will likely live a longer, happier life and be easier to care for. Here are some key signs to look for when selecting your leopard gecko:

First, check the gecko's eyes and nostrils. A healthy leopard gecko will have clear, bright eyes with no discharge. The eyes should look alert and clean. Similarly, the nostrils should be free of mucus or any other substances. If you notice any discharge from the eyes or nose, this could indicate respiratory problems or illness, and it might be best to choose a different gecko.

Next, observe the gecko's behavior. Leopard geckos are generally calm and may be a bit shy, but they should still show some curiosity and activity, especially during the evening or nighttime when they are more naturally active. If the gecko seems very lethargic, uninterested in its surroundings, or unwilling to move, this could be a sign that something is wrong. A healthy gecko will be alert and responsive, showing interest in its environment.

The gecko's skin and tail are also important indicators of health. The skin should be smooth and free of any sores, scars, or patches of old skin that haven't shed properly. Retained shed can lead to health issues, so it's important that the gecko's skin is in good condition. The tail is particularly significant because leopard geckos store fat in their tails, which helps them stay healthy. A plump, thick tail usually means the gecko is well-fed and in good health. On the other hand, a thin or shriveled tail might suggest the gecko is malnourished or sick.

Lastly, it's a good idea to ask the seller if you can watch the gecko eat. A healthy leopard gecko should be eager to eat live insects like crickets or mealworms. If the gecko shows little interest in food or refuses to eat, this could be a red flag that it's not well.

☐ Different Morphs And Colors

When it comes to choosing a leopard gecko, one of the most exciting parts is picking out your favorite "morph." A morph refers to the different colors and patterns that a leopard gecko can have. Over the years, breeders have developed many different morphs, giving you plenty of options to choose from. These range from the classic yellow and black spotted pattern that most people recognize to unique and rare colors like albino, tangerine, or even all-white geckos.

Let's start with the Classic or Wild-Type leopard gecko. This is the most common type and is yellow with black spots. If you picture a leopard gecko, this is likely the image that comes to mind. It's the natural look of a leopard gecko in the wild and remains a popular choice for many pet owners.

Next is the Albino leopard gecko. These geckos are special because they lack the dark pigments that create the black spots seen in the wild-type. Instead, their skin is lighter and often has a pinkish tint. There are several kinds of albino morphs, each with its own unique look. These geckos are particularly eye-catching because of their soft, light-colored appearance.

The Tangerine morph is another popular option. These geckos have a bright, orange color that can range from a light, soft orange to a deep, almost red hue. Their vibrant color makes them stand out and they're a favorite among those who want a gecko that's a bit more flashy.

Blizzard leopard geckos are quite different from the classic look. These geckos are solid-colored, without the spots that are typical in other morphs. They can be white, yellow, or even have a purplish-gray color. The absence of a pattern gives them a unique, clean look that many people find appealing.

Lastly, there are Patternless leopard geckos. As the name suggests, these geckos have no pattern at all. They are typically a solid color that can range from yellow to greenish tones. This morph is great for those who prefer a more uniform look in their pet.

Where To Buy: Breeders Vs. Pet Stores

When you're ready to bring a leopard gecko into your home, the next step is deciding where to buy it. You generally have two main options: buying from a breeder or purchasing from a pet store. Each option has its advantages and disadvantages, so it's important to consider both before making your decision.

Breeders:

Buying from a breeder is often the best choice if you're looking for a specific type of leopard gecko or if you want to ensure your gecko is healthy. Breeders usually have extensive knowledge about the geckos they raise and can provide detailed information about their care, genetics, and health history. This knowledge helps you understand what to expect with your new pet and ensures you're getting a well-cared-for animal. Additionally, breeders are more likely to offer ongoing support after your purchase. If you have any questions or concerns about your gecko, a breeder is often willing to help. However, one downside is that buying from a breeder can be more expensive, especially if you're interested in a rare or unique morph.

Pet Stores:

On the other hand, pet stores can be a more convenient option, especially if you prefer to see and choose your gecko in person. Pet stores are widely available, and you can often find a leopard gecko without much hassle. However, there are some potential drawbacks to consider. The quality of care in pet stores can vary greatly. In some cases, the geckos may not receive the best care, which can lead to health issues. Additionally, the staff at pet stores might not have specialized knowledge about leopard geckos, making it harder to get accurate information about their care. If you decide to buy from a pet store, it's important to carefully observe the conditions the geckos are kept in. Look for signs that the animals are healthy and ask the staff about how they care for the geckos.

CHAPTER THREE

SETTING UP THE PERFECT ENCLOSURE

Enclosure Types And Sizes

Selecting the right enclosure for your leopard gecko is key to keeping them healthy and happy. Leopard geckos thrive in environments that closely resemble their natural habitat. Here's a guide to help you choose the best enclosure for your pet:

1. Glass Terrariums or Aquariums:

A glass terrarium or aquarium is the most popular choice for housing leopard geckos. Glass enclosures are easy to clean and offer a clear view of your gecko. For one leopard gecko, a 20-gallon long terrarium, which measures 30 inches long, 12 inches wide, and 12 inches high, is usually adequate. If you plan to keep more than one gecko or want to give your gecko more room to explore, consider using a larger enclosure. Options like a 40-gallon or 75-gallon terrarium provide extra space and can make your gecko's environment more stimulating.

2. Plastic Enclosures:

Plastic enclosures, made from materials like polypropylene, are another option. These enclosures are typically lighter and easier to handle compared to glass. They can be a good choice if you need to move the enclosure frequently or want something more portable. However, ensure the plastic is strong enough to hold heat and won't easily crack or break.

3. Custom Cages:

For a more personalized setup, you can use custom-built enclosures made from materials such as wood or metal. Custom cages offer flexibility in terms of size and design. Just make sure that any materials used are safe for reptiles and that the enclosure has good ventilation to keep your gecko's environment healthy.

Important Considerations:

Regardless of the type of enclosure you choose, it's essential that it is secure. Check for any gaps or openings where your gecko could escape. Proper ventilation is also crucial to prevent overheating and ensure your gecko remains comfortable. Additionally, the enclosure should be easy to clean to maintain a healthy environment for your pet.

Substrate Options: Pros And Cons

Choosing the right substrate for your leopard gecko is essential for their health and comfort. Here are some common options and their benefits and drawbacks:

Reptile Carpet: Reptile carpets are a popular choice among leopard gecko owners. They are made from a washable, non-toxic material that is easy to clean. The carpet provides a soft surface that is gentle on your gecko's feet. Additionally, it helps control humidity levels in the enclosure, which is beneficial for your gecko's health. One of the main advantages of reptile carpet is that it reduces the risk of impaction, which occurs when a gecko ingests substrate that blocks their digestive system.

Paper Towels or Newspaper: Paper towels and newspaper are cost-effective and simple to use. They are easy to replace and clean, making them a practical choice for many pet owners. These options also help you keep an eye on your gecko's droppings, which is useful for monitoring their health. However, paper towels and newspaper don't offer a natural look or feel and may need to be changed frequently to maintain cleanliness.

Sand: Sand can create a natural desert-like environment for your leopard gecko. It can be visually appealing and mimic the gecko's natural habitat. However, sand carries a risk of causing impaction if your gecko ingests it. To minimize this risk, make sure you use sand specifically designed for reptiles and avoid using sand from hardware stores or beaches. Regularly cleaning and monitoring the sand is crucial to prevent any health issues.

Loose Substrates (e.g., Coconut Fiber or Reptile Soil): Loose substrates such as coconut fiber or reptile soil provide a more natural environment for your leopard gecko. They can retain moisture well, which is beneficial for maintaining proper humidity levels. These substrates can also offer a more realistic habitat for your gecko. However, loose substrates require regular cleaning and replacement to avoid mold and bacteria growth, which can pose health risks to your pet.

When choosing a substrate, it is important to avoid any material that could be ingested and cause impaction. The substrate should be easy to clean and safe for your gecko's health.

Temperature And Lighting Requirements

Keeping your leopard gecko healthy involves managing their temperature and lighting correctly. These reptiles are ectothermic, which means they rely on external heat to regulate their body temperature. Here's how you can create a suitable environment for them:

Temperature: Leopard geckos need a temperature gradient in their habitat. This means you should have both a warm and a cool side in their enclosure. During the day, the warm side should be between 88-92°F (31-33°C). This warmth helps them digest their food and stay active. The cool side should be around 75-80°F (24-27°C). This gradient allows your gecko to move between different temperatures based on their needs. To maintain these temperatures, use a reliable thermometer to keep track. Place a heat mat or heat tape under one side of the enclosure to create the warm side. Avoid using hot rocks for heating as they can become too hot and cause burns.

Lighting: Leopard geckos are nocturnal, meaning they are active at night and sleep during the day. They don't need strong UVB lighting like some other reptiles, but a low-intensity UVB light can still be beneficial for their overall health. This light should be on for about 10-12 hours a day to mimic a natural day-night cycle. You can use a simple light source, such as a low-wattage incandescent bulb, to maintain a regular schedule for your gecko. This helps in keeping their natural rhythm and promotes overall well-being.

Humidity: Although not a primary concern, it is important to manage humidity levels to ensure your leopard gecko's comfort. They come from arid environments, so the humidity in their enclosure should be relatively low. Aim for a humidity level of around 30-40%. Providing a moist hide, which is a small box filled with damp substrate, can help with shedding and give your gecko a comfortable spot to retreat to. This moist hide ensures they can keep their skin in good condition and helps them shed properly.

CHAPTER FOUR

HEATING AND HUMIDITY

Ideal Temperature Ranges

Leopard geckos come from the dry, warm regions of Asia, so it's important to recreate their natural habitat in captivity to keep them healthy and happy. Maintaining the right temperature in their enclosure is key to their well-being.

During the day, leopard geckos do best in temperatures between 75°F and 85°F (24°C to 29°C). These temperatures mimic their natural daytime environment. At night, it's fine for the temperature to drop a bit, ideally to between 65°F and 75°F (18°C to 24°C). This nighttime cool-down helps mimic their natural habitat's temperature variations.

To create the best environment for your leopard gecko, set up a temperature gradient in their habitat. This means having a warm side and a cooler side within the enclosure. This gradient allows your gecko to move to different parts of the habitat to regulate their body temperature as needed.

For the warm side of the enclosure, maintain temperatures between 85°F and 90°F (29°C to 32°C). This warmer area is where your gecko can bask and get the heat it needs to stay active and digest food properly. The warm side should have a heat source, like a heat mat or heat lamp, to achieve and maintain these temperatures.

On the other hand, the cool side of the enclosure should be around 75°F (24°C). This cooler area provides a place for your gecko to retreat when it needs to lower its body temperature. It's important that the cool side is not too cold, as leopard geckos need to stay within their ideal temperature range to stay healthy.

By creating this temperature gradient, you ensure that your leopard gecko can choose the best spot to regulate its body heat. This setup helps prevent stress and health issues related to improper temperature. Regularly check the temperatures in both areas using reliable thermometers to ensure that your gecko's habitat remains within the ideal range.

Using Heat Mats And Lamps

To keep your leopard gecko healthy and comfortable, you need to provide the right temperature in its enclosure. Heat mats and heat lamps are two effective tools for achieving this.

Heat Mats: Heat mats, also called under-tank heaters, are placed under one side of the tank. They create a warm spot, which is essential for your gecko's digestion and activity. These mats offer a steady, consistent heat source. When setting up a heat mat, make sure it's the right size for your tank. Always place it under the tank, not inside it, to avoid direct contact with your gecko. This setup helps maintain a warm area without causing harm.

Heat Lamps: Heat lamps are another way to provide warmth and are particularly useful if you need to quickly increase the temperature in the tank. You can mount the lamp above the enclosure so it creates a basking area on one side. Position the lamp carefully to ensure that it heats up only one part of the tank, allowing your gecko to move to cooler areas if needed. Be cautious with heat lamps because they can get very hot. Ensure the lamp is securely mounted to prevent it from falling or being knocked over, and use a cover to prevent your gecko from coming into direct contact with the lamp.

Monitoring Temperature: Regardless of whether you use heat mats or lamps, it's crucial to monitor the temperature closely. Place a reliable thermometer in both the warm and cool sides of the tank to keep track of temperature changes. Avoid using glass thermometers, as they can be inaccurate. Instead, opt for digital thermometers with remote probes. These provide precise temperature readings and help you ensure your gecko's environment remains within the optimal range.

Maintaining Proper Humidity Levels

Even though leopard geckos come from dry environments, they still need the right amount of humidity to stay healthy. The best humidity range for these geckos is between 30% and 40%. Proper humidity helps them shed their skin correctly and keeps their skin in good condition.

To manage humidity in your gecko's habitat, you'll need a few tools and methods. A hygrometer is essential. This device measures the humidity level inside the tank. Place the hygrometer inside the enclosure to keep track of how moist the air is.

If the humidity drops below the ideal range, you can use a spray bottle to mist the tank lightly a few times a week. This will add moisture to the air and help your gecko shed its skin properly. Be careful not to overdo it, as too much moisture can cause problems like fungal infections. The enclosure should be moist but not wet.

A humid hide is another important tool. This is a small, enclosed area within the tank where your gecko can go to find higher humidity. You can create a humid hide by filling it with damp sphagnum moss or paper towels. This helps provide a moist spot for your gecko to go to when it needs extra humidity. Check the humid hide regularly to make sure it stays damp but not soggy.

Proper ventilation is also crucial for managing humidity. Good airflow prevents too much moisture from building up, which can lead to mold and other problems. Make sure your enclosure has small gaps or vents to allow air to circulate freely. This helps keep the environment comfortable and reduces the risk of humidity-related issues.

☐

CHAPTER FIVE

FEEDING YOUR LEOPARD GECKO

Feeding Your Leopard Gecko

Leopard geckos need a diet mainly consisting of live insects. These insects are vital for their growth and health. The best insects to feed your gecko include crickets, mealworms, and dubia roaches. These options are rich in protein and provide the nutrients your gecko needs. You can also occasionally give waxworms and hornworms as treats.

When feeding your gecko, it's important to choose insects that are the right size. The insects should be no bigger than the width of your gecko's head. For young geckos, this means offering smaller insects, while adult geckos can handle larger ones.

In addition to providing insects, it's essential to give your gecko dietary supplements. Calcium is crucial for maintaining healthy bones and preventing diseases like metabolic bone disease. To ensure your gecko gets enough calcium, you need to dust the insects with a calcium supplement. Vitamin D3 is also important because it helps your gecko absorb calcium. You can find calcium supplements with added Vitamin D3 at pet stores or online.

To use the supplements, dust the insects just before feeding. Place a small amount of the powdered supplement in a container, add the insects, and gently shake the container to coat the insects evenly. This ensures that your gecko receives the necessary nutrients with each meal.

☐

Feeding Schedule And Portion Control

Maintaining a regular feeding schedule is key to keeping your gecko healthy and happy. For juvenile geckos—those under six months old—it's best to feed them every day. As your gecko grows, you can cut back on the frequency of feedings. Adult geckos usually thrive with feedings every other day or every three days.

Portion control is also crucial to prevent problems like obesity. The amount of food your gecko needs varies based on its size and age. A practical guideline is to offer your gecko as many insects as it can eat in 10 to 15 minutes. After this time, remove any leftover insects. This helps avoid overfeeding and keeps the habitat clean.

Keep an eye on your gecko's weight and overall health regularly. If you notice that your gecko is gaining too much weight or seems too thin, you should adjust how much and how often you feed it. Making these adjustments ensures your gecko remains in good shape.

It's important to remember that every gecko is different. Their dietary needs can change based on their activity level, metabolism, and specific health conditions. If you're ever unsure about what's best for your gecko, don't hesitate to consult a reptile veterinarian. They can provide advice tailored to your gecko's needs and help you make informed decisions about its diet.

☐

Gut-Loading And Dusting Insects

Feeding your gecko nutritious insects is essential for its health, and two important steps can help ensure your pet gets the most out of its meals: gut-loading and dusting.

What is Gut-Loading?

Gut-loading is a process where you feed the insects a healthy diet before giving them to your gecko. The idea is that by feeding the insects nutritious foods, like vegetables, fruits, and high-quality insect food, these nutrients will be passed on to your gecko when it eats the insects.

Here's how you can do it: A day before you plan to feed the insects to your gecko, provide them with a variety of nutritious foods. This could include fresh vegetables such as carrots or leafy greens, fruits like apples or bananas, and specially formulated insect foods. By doing this, you are making sure that the insects are well-fed and packed with essential vitamins and minerals.

Why is Gut-Loading Important?

Gut-loading helps improve the nutritional value of the insects. When your gecko consumes these insects, it benefits from the additional nutrients they carry. This means your gecko gets more of the vitamins and minerals it needs to stay healthy, which can lead to better overall well-being and vitality.

What is Dusting?

In addition to gut-loading, dusting the insects with supplements is another important step. Dusting means coating the insects with a fine powder that contains calcium and vitamins. This is crucial because it ensures that your gecko receives extra nutrients that might not be fully available through gut-loading alone.

To dust the insects, use a calcium and vitamin powder specifically designed for reptiles. Gently shake the powder over the insects or place the insects and powder in a container and shake them together. Make sure each insect is evenly coated with the powder.

Why is Dusting Important?

Dusting helps prevent nutritional deficiencies by providing extra calcium and vitamins that are vital for your gecko's health. Calcium is especially important for bone health and preventing conditions like metabolic bone disease. Vitamins support overall health and immune function.

CHAPTER SIX

WATER AND HYDRATION

Providing Fresh Water

Keeping your leopard gecko healthy requires providing fresh, clean water every day. Despite their natural habitat being dry, leopard geckos still need proper hydration to stay well. Here's how to ensure your gecko always has access to fresh water:

Daily Water Supply

Leopard geckos need fresh water every day. Place a shallow dish in their enclosure where they can easily reach it. The dish should be big enough for your gecko to drink from but not so deep that it becomes a risk for drowning.

Dish Selection

Use a ceramic or plastic dish for the water. These materials are easy to clean and won't rust, unlike metal dishes, which can affect the water quality. Make sure the dish is clean and free from any debris before filling it.

Dish Placement

Position the water dish in a spot where it won't get too hot. Extreme temperatures can cause the water to evaporate quickly, leaving your gecko without a proper water supply. Ideally, place it in a cool area of the enclosure where it's easy for your gecko to find.

Daily Maintenance

Change the water at least once a day. This helps prevent bacteria from growing and ensures the water remains clean. If the water dish has any residue or algae, clean it thoroughly. Use warm water and a mild soap to scrub the dish, then rinse it well to remove any soap residue before adding fresh water.

Monitoring and Cleaning

Regularly check the water dish to ensure it's in good condition and the water is clean. If you see any signs of algae or dirt, clean the dish immediately. Keeping the water fresh and the dish clean is essential for your leopard gecko's health.

How To Monitor Hydration Levels

Keeping an eye on your leopard gecko's hydration is crucial for their health. Unlike some pets that show obvious signs of being thirsty, leopard geckos can be a bit more subtle. Here's how to monitor their hydration and ensure they're getting enough water:

1. Check Their Skin

The condition of your gecko's skin is a good indicator of their hydration. A healthy, well-hydrated leopard gecko will have smooth and plump skin. If you notice that their skin is looking wrinkled, dry, or loose, it might be a sign they're not drinking enough water. Dry, flaky skin can be a red flag for dehydration, so be sure to check their skin regularly.

2. Observe Their Behavior

Your leopard gecko's activity levels can also give you clues about their hydration status. Normally, geckos are fairly active and curious. If you see that your gecko is unusually lethargic or seems less active than usual, it could be because they're not getting enough water. A sudden drop in energy or a noticeable change in their behavior might indicate they need more hydration.

3. Examine Their Droppings

The consistency of your gecko's droppings is another important factor. Healthy droppings should be well-formed and not excessively dry. If you find that their feces are dry and hard, it could be a sign that they're not properly hydrated. Make it a habit to observe their droppings to ensure they are consistent with normal, healthy waste.

4. Monitor Their Weight

Keeping track of your leopard gecko's weight is essential for spotting health issues, including dehydration. Sudden weight loss can be a warning sign that something is wrong. Use a scale that can measure small changes accurately, and weigh your gecko regularly. Any significant or rapid weight loss should be addressed promptly, as it might indicate a problem with their hydration or overall health.

Signs Of Dehydration

Keeping an eye on your leopard gecko's health is essential, and recognizing the signs of dehydration can help you act quickly to prevent more serious issues. Here's how to spot dehydration in your gecko:

1.   Sunken Eyes: One of the most obvious signs of dehydration is when your

gecko's eyes look sunken or dull. Healthy gecko eyes should be bright and clear. If they appear sunken or cloudy, it's a sign that your gecko might not be getting enough water.

2. Dry Skin: Check your gecko's skin regularly. If it feels dry or rough, this could mean they're dehydrated. Healthy gecko skin should be smooth and slightly moist. Dry skin can indicate that they're not drinking enough water.

3. Lethargy: Dehydration can make your gecko feel weak and less active. If your gecko seems unusually tired, sluggish, or isn't moving around as much as usual, dehydration might be the cause. Active geckos that suddenly become lethargic could be experiencing dehydration.

4.　Loss of Appetite: A gecko that is dehydrated might eat less or refuse food altogether. If you notice that your gecko isn't eating as much as usual or is ignoring food, it might be because they are not properly hydrated.

5.　Difficulty Shedding: Proper hydration is crucial for healthy shedding. If your gecko is having trouble shedding their skin or has incomplete sheds, dehydration could be the reason. When geckos don't get enough water, their skin can become too dry, making shedding difficult.

If you see any of these signs, it's important to take action right away. Start by ensuring your gecko has access to fresh water at all times. You might also want to lightly mist their habitat to increase the humidity, which can help with hydration.

For severe symptoms or if your gecko's condition doesn't improve, it's best to consult a veterinarian who specializes in reptiles. They can provide a thorough examination and recommend the best treatment for your gecko's health.

CHAPTER SEVEN

HANDLING AND SOCIALIZATION

Safe Handling Techniques

Handling your Leopard Gecko safely is essential for both your gecko's health and your own comfort. These reptiles are generally calm and can get used to being handled with some patience and the right techniques. Follow these simple steps to handle your gecko safely:

1. Wash Your Hands: Before and after handling your gecko, make sure to wash your hands thoroughly. This practice helps prevent transferring any harmful substances to your gecko and reduces the risk of spreading bacteria.

2. Approach Slowly: Leopard Geckos can be a bit skittish. To avoid startling them,

approach slowly and gently. Quick or sudden movements might frighten your gecko, causing it stress or defensive reactions.

3. Support Their Body: When picking up your gecko, use both hands to support its whole body. Gently scoop them up from underneath, making sure they feel secure. Avoid grabbing them by the tail, as this can hurt them or make them anxious.

4. Keep Handling Sessions Short: In the beginning, keep handling sessions brief, just a few minutes at a time. This helps your gecko get used to the process without becoming overwhelmed. As your gecko becomes more comfortable, you can gradually increase the time you spend handling them.

5. Use a Flat Surface: If you're unsure about picking up your gecko, you can place them on a flat, secure surface like a table. Gently guide your gecko onto the surface and let them explore at their own pace. This can help both you and your gecko get used to handling in a less stressful way.

6. Watch Their Body Language: Pay close attention to your gecko's body language. If your gecko appears stressed, such as by flicking its tail rapidly, hiding, or making noises, stay calm and gently place them back in their habitat. Observing these signs will help you respond appropriately and ensure your gecko remains comfortable.

Building Trust With Your Gecko

Building a trusting relationship with your Leopard Gecko is a process that requires patience, consistency, and gentle care.

Here's a simple guide to help you build trust with your gecko:

1. Stick to a Routine: Geckos are creatures of habit. To help your gecko feel secure, establish a regular routine for feeding and handling. Consistency in these activities helps your gecko know what to expect, which makes them feel more comfortable around you.

2. Use Positive Reinforcement: Offer your gecko treats or their favorite foods as a reward when they behave calmly during handling. Positive reinforcement helps your gecko associate your presence with good things, making them more likely to trust you.

3. Handle Gently: Always handle your gecko with care. Avoid making sudden

movements, as this can startle them. Speak to them in a soft, soothing voice. Your calm demeanor and gentle touch will help your gecko feel safe and less anxious.

4. Respect Their Space: Give your gecko time to adjust to being handled. If your gecko seems stressed or uncomfortable, let them go and try again later. Forcing interaction can create fear and mistrust, so it's important to be patient and allow your gecko to approach you on their own terms.

5. Provide Enrichment: Make sure your gecko has plenty of things to do in their habitat. Adding new hiding spots, climbing structures, and other enrichment activities can help your gecko feel more secure and less stressed. A well-enriched environment supports your gecko's overall well-being

and makes them more comfortable interacting with you.

Understanding Gecko Behavior

Knowing how Leopard Geckos behave helps you handle and interact with them better. These reptiles have specific behaviors that can tell you a lot about how they're feeling and their comfort level.

Tail Movements: One of the most important indicators of a Leopard Gecko's mood is its tail. When a gecko's tail is relaxed and held in a neutral position, it usually means the gecko is comfortable and content. However, if the tail is rapidly flicking or puffed up, it can be a sign that the gecko is feeling stressed or agitated. Pay attention to these tail movements to gauge how your gecko is feeling.

Hiding: Leopard Geckos are natural hiders. It's common for them to retreat to their hiding spots, especially if they feel threatened or need some alone time. If your gecko is hiding, it's important to give them space and allow them to come out when they feel safe. This behavior is perfectly normal and indicates that the gecko is responding to its environment.

Exploration: These geckos are curious creatures and enjoy exploring their surroundings. They benefit from having a habitat with various textures and hiding spots. This variety encourages natural behaviors and helps keep them from becoming stressed. By providing different elements in their habitat, you support their natural instincts and contribute to their well-being.

Feeding Response: How your gecko reacts during feeding times can give you clues about their health and mood. A healthy leopard gecko will usually have a good appetite and be eager to eat. If your gecko is less interested in food or doesn't eat as much as usual, it could be a sign of stress or a potential health problem. Regular feeding responses are a good indicator of overall health.

Basking and Activity: Leopard Geckos need to regulate their body temperature, so they will bask under heat sources to stay warm. Observing how your gecko basks can help you ensure that their habitat has the right temperature range. Activity levels can vary from gecko to gecko. Some may be more active at night (as they are nocturnal), while others may have different patterns of activity throughout the day.

CHAPTER EIGHT

HEALTH AND WELLNESS

Common Health Issues

Leopard geckos are generally strong and healthy reptiles, but they can face some common health issues. Understanding these problems can help you keep your gecko happy and well.

Metabolic Bone Disease (MBD) is a common issue that often happens when a leopard gecko doesn't get enough calcium and vitamin D3 in its diet. This disease affects the bones, making them weak and misshapen. You might notice signs like soft or crooked bones, difficulty moving, or a reduced appetite. If your gecko has these symptoms, it's important to adjust its diet and seek veterinary help.

Parasites are another concern. These can be internal, like worms, or external, like mites. Internal parasites can cause weight loss, diarrhea, and a lack of appetite. External parasites, such as mites, are tiny bugs that can irritate the skin, causing itching or redness. Regular check-ups and good hygiene can help prevent and treat these issues.

Impaction occurs when a gecko swallows something that it can't digest, like sand or small particles from its habitat. This blockage can lead to severe discomfort, lethargy, and constipation. If you suspect impaction, it's crucial to remove the indigestible material and consult a vet for treatment.

Respiratory Infections are often caused by improper heating or humidity levels in your gecko's enclosure. Symptoms include wheezing, difficulty breathing, and nasal discharge. These infections need to be treated quickly to avoid more serious health problems. Make sure the habitat is correctly heated and humidified to prevent these issues.

Tail Rot is a condition where the tissue in a gecko's tail starts to die. This can happen due to injuries or poor living conditions. The tail might turn black, become soft, and could eventually fall off if not treated. Proper care and a clean environment can help prevent tail rot. If your gecko's tail shows signs of rot, seek veterinary advice right away.

Signs Of Illness To Watch For

Recognizing signs of illness in your gecko early is crucial for their well-being. By paying close attention to their behavior and physical condition, you can help ensure a quicker recovery if they become unwell. Here are some common signs of illness to watch for:

Change in Appetite: If your gecko suddenly stops eating or shows no interest in food, it could be a sign of a health issue. Geckos typically have a good appetite, so if yours isn't eating for more than a couple of days, it's important to investigate the cause.

Lethargy: Geckos do spend a lot of time resting and sleeping. However, if your gecko appears unusually tired, sluggish, or unresponsive, it may be a sign of a health problem. If their energy levels seem much lower than usual or they are not moving around as much, it could indicate an underlying issue.

Abnormal Feces: Pay attention to your gecko's droppings. Diarrhea, a lack of bowel movements, or any changes in the color or consistency of their feces can signal digestive problems or parasitic infections. Regular monitoring of their waste can provide valuable clues about their health.

Changes in Skin or Tail: Check your gecko's skin and tail regularly. Unusual changes such as discoloration, sores, or swelling might indicate infections or other health issues. Healthy skin should be smooth and free of bumps or lesions. Any visible changes could be a sign that something is wrong.

Difficulty Breathing: If your gecko is having trouble breathing, such as wheezing, gasping, or having nasal discharge, it could be suffering from a respiratory infection. Healthy geckos should breathe easily and quietly. Any signs of labored breathing or abnormal respiratory sounds should be addressed promptly.

Weight Loss: Unexplained weight loss can be a warning sign of various health issues. This might include parasites, poor diet, or internal problems. If your gecko is losing weight without any clear reason, it's essential to investigate further.

☐ When To Visit The Vet

Taking care of your leopard gecko means knowing when it's time to see a veterinarian. Here's a guide to help you decide when a vet visit is necessary:

Persistent Symptoms

If your leopard gecko shows signs of illness, such as changes in eating habits, unusual behavior, or abnormal skin conditions, and these symptoms last more than a few days, it's important to consult a veterinarian. Persistent symptoms often indicate that something is wrong and requires professional attention. Delaying a vet visit could result in the condition worsening, so it's best to seek help if the problem doesn't resolve quickly.

Severe Conditions

In some cases, the symptoms your gecko displays might be more serious. For instance, if you notice significant weight loss, severe difficulty breathing, or visible signs of distress, it's crucial to take your gecko to the vet right away. Severe conditions can be life-threatening and need immediate medical attention. Quick action can make a big difference in your gecko's recovery and overall health.

Preventive Care

Even if your leopard gecko appears to be healthy, regular check-ups with a reptile veterinarian are a good practice. Annual health exams can help catch potential issues before they become serious problems. Preventive care is essential for maintaining your gecko's health and ensuring they are thriving. A vet can provide valuable advice on diet, habitat, and general care, helping to keep your gecko in the best possible condition.

Uncertainty

If you're ever unsure about your gecko's health or have questions about their behavior or condition, don't hesitate to consult a veterinarian. Sometimes, what might seem like a minor issue could be a sign of a more significant problem. A vet can offer guidance and give you peace of mind, confirming whether your gecko is healthy or if further action is needed. It's always better to be cautious and get professional advice when in doubt.

CHAPTER NINE

SHEDDING AND SKIN CARE

Understanding The Shedding Process

Shedding, or ecdysis, is a natural and essential part of a leopard gecko's life. This process allows the gecko to grow and get rid of old, worn-out skin. Like all reptiles, leopard geckos shed their skin regularly. For young geckos and hatchlings, shedding happens every few weeks. As they get older, adults will shed their skin every few months. Knowing about this process can help you take better care of your gecko.

Before a leopard gecko sheds, you'll notice some signs. Its skin might look dull or cloudy, and its colors may seem less bright. This cloudiness happens because of a fluid that builds up between the old skin and the new skin growing underneath. As the shedding process starts, the gecko will look for a place that helps with shedding, often rubbing against rough surfaces to help remove the old skin.

During shedding, the gecko may become more secretive or inactive. It might spend more time hiding or resting. This behavior is normal and part of its effort to shed the old skin comfortably. Providing a suitable environment for your gecko can make this process easier. A humidity box or a moist hide area can be very helpful. This box should be filled with damp moss or paper towels, which help keep the gecko's skin moist and make shedding smoother.

If you notice your gecko struggling with shedding or if parts of the old skin are stuck, it's important to help. You can gently mist the gecko with water or place it in a humid box to help loosen the stuck skin. Be careful not to pull at the old skin yourself, as this can cause injury. If you're unsure or if the problem persists, consult a veterinarian who specializes in reptiles.

After shedding, the gecko's skin will look fresh and vibrant. It's also a good time to check for any signs of skin issues or injuries. Regular shedding is a sign of good health in leopard geckos. By understanding this process and providing the right environment, you can help ensure that your gecko remains healthy and comfortable.

How To Help With Stuck Shed

Leopard geckos sometimes have trouble shedding their skin, which can leave old skin stuck to them. This is especially common around sensitive areas like their toes and tail. If your gecko has stuck shed, it can be uncomfortable and might lead to health problems if not addressed. Here's what you can do to help:

1.   Maintain Proper Humidity: Leopard geckos need a specific level of humidity to shed their skin properly. Make sure your gecko's habitat has the right amount of moisture. One way to ensure proper humidity is by providing a moist hide. This can be a small box or container lined with damp paper towels or sphagnum moss. Your gecko can use this hide to help with shedding.

2.   Soak Your Gecko: If your gecko has stuck shed, a gentle soak can help loosen the old skin. Fill a shallow dish with warm water (not hot) and place your gecko in it

for about 10 to 15 minutes. The water should be shallow enough so your gecko can't fully submerge itself, as being too deep might stress them.

3.   Gently Assist: After soaking, you can help your gecko remove the stuck shed carefully. Use a soft, damp cloth or a cotton swab to gently rub the areas where the old skin is stuck. Avoid pulling or tugging at the skin, as this can hurt your gecko. If you're unsure about how to do this safely, it's a good idea to consult a reptile veterinarian for advice.

4.   Watch for Health Issues: After dealing with stuck shed, keep an eye on your gecko. Look out for signs of infection, such as redness or swelling. Also, monitor your gecko for unusual stress or lethargy. If you notice any concerning symptoms or if

your gecko isn't improving, seek veterinary help promptly.

Preventing Shedding Problems

Shedding is a natural process for leopard geckos, but problems can arise if certain conditions aren't met. To ensure your gecko sheds properly and stays healthy, follow these simple guidelines:

1. Keep the Right Humidity: Proper humidity is crucial for a smooth shedding process. Leopard geckos need a humidity level of around 30-40%. To help maintain this, include a humid hide in your gecko's enclosure. This special hide provides a moist environment that supports the shedding process, allowing your gecko to help remove its old skin more easily.

2. Create a Suitable Habitat: Make sure your gecko's home has the right surfaces

for shedding. Rough surfaces, like rocks or branches, are ideal because they help your gecko rub off old skin. Avoid using overly smooth surfaces, as they may not be as effective in aiding the shedding process. A well-arranged habitat can make a big difference in how smoothly your gecko sheds.

3. Provide a Balanced Diet: A healthy diet is essential for maintaining good skin. Feed your leopard gecko a variety of insects, such as crickets and mealworms, and consider adding supplements to ensure it receives all the necessary nutrients. Proper nutrition supports skin health and can help prevent shedding issues.

4. Perform Regular Health Checks: Regularly examine your gecko for any signs

of shedding problems or other health concerns. By keeping an eye on your gecko's skin and behavior, you can catch potential issues early. This proactive approach allows you to address any problems before they become more serious.

5. Minimize Handling: Handling your leopard gecko is important for bonding, but avoid excessive handling, especially during or right after shedding. Too much handling can stress your gecko and interfere with the shedding process. Allow your gecko to shed in a calm environment without additional stress.

CHAPTER TEN

BREEDING BASICS

Introduction To Breeding Leopard Geckos

Breeding Leopard Geckos can be both exciting and rewarding, but it's important to be well-prepared. These geckos are popular pets because of their beautiful colors and patterns, but breeding them requires careful planning and attention to detail.

Leopard Geckos are easier to breed than some other reptiles, but successful breeding involves more than just pairing a male and female. To start, you need to create the right environment for them. This means setting up a suitable habitat with proper heating, lighting, and humidity. The right conditions are crucial for the health of the geckos and the success of the breeding process.

Understanding the reproductive cycle of Leopard Geckos is also essential. The breeding season typically starts in the spring. During this time, you should introduce the male and female geckos in a controlled manner. Monitor their interactions to ensure they are compatible and not aggressive towards each other. It's normal for the male to display mating behaviors such as tail-waving and chirping.

Once mating occurs, the female will lay eggs. These eggs need to be carefully managed to ensure they hatch successfully. Leopard Gecko eggs are usually laid in a pair, and they need to be kept in a warm, humid environment to incubate. You should place the eggs in a suitable incubator or a container with a moist substrate. The ideal temperature for incubating Leopard Gecko eggs is between 80-85°F (27-29°C). The eggs will typically hatch after about 45-60 days, depending on the temperature and humidity.

After the eggs hatch, you'll need to provide proper care for the hatchlings. Leopard Gecko babies are tiny and require a safe, warm, and moist environment. They will need a proper diet, which typically includes small insects like pinhead crickets or fruit flies. Ensure they have access to clean water and are housed in a suitable enclosure with proper heating.

Preparing For Breeding Season

Successful breeding starts with careful preparation. Here are some guides to help you get ready for the breeding season with your Leopard Geckos:

1. Choose Healthy Geckos: Before you start, make sure both your male and female Leopard Geckos are healthy. They should be free from diseases, parasites, and any signs of illness. Healthy geckos are more likely to produce strong and healthy offspring.

2. Check Their Age: Leopard Geckos usually become sexually mature at around 18 months to 2 years old. Breeding them before they reach this age can cause health problems for both the geckos and their babies. Ensure your geckos are of the right age before beginning the breeding process.

3. Set Up a Breeding Environment: Create a separate breeding enclosure that

mimics the natural conditions Leopard Geckos are used to. This enclosure should have appropriate temperature gradients, humidity levels, and plenty of hiding spots. Keep the enclosure clean and safe from any potential dangers.

4. Manage Temperature and Lighting: Leopard Geckos need a temperature gradient in their enclosure to stay healthy. During the breeding season, increase the temperature slightly to encourage reproductive activity. Aim for a daytime temperature of around 85-90°F and a nighttime temperature of 70-75°F. While UV lighting isn't essential, providing a regular day/night light cycle helps regulate their internal clocks.

5. Provide a Balanced Diet: Make sure both your male and female Leopard Geckos

are well-fed before breeding. A nutritious diet rich in protein, calcium, and vitamins is important for their health and reproductive success. Offer a variety of foods, such as crickets and mealworms, and consider adding occasional supplements to their diet.

6. Introduce the Geckos: Once everything is prepared, you can introduce the male and female Leopard Geckos. Keep a close eye on their behavior to ensure they get along and don't show any signs of aggression. It's often best to place the female in the male's enclosure rather than the other way around to reduce any territorial disputes.

Caring For Eggs And Hatchlings

Once a female Leopard Gecko mates, she will lay eggs that need special care to ensure they hatch successfully. Here are some simple guides to help you through the process:

1. Egg-Laying Process: After mating, the female will lay eggs about 20 to 30 days later. She typically lays 2 to 3 eggs per clutch, and she may lay multiple clutches over a few months. To encourage egg-laying, provide a suitable laying area in her enclosure. This area should have a moist substrate like vermiculite or perlite. This helps her feel comfortable and increases the chances of successful egg-laying.

2. Collecting Eggs: When the eggs are laid, gently remove them from the enclosure. Use a spoon or similar tool to lift them carefully, avoiding turning or shaking them, as this can harm the developing embryos inside. Place the eggs in an

incubator or a container with a moist substrate that's specifically designed for incubation.

3. Incubation: The eggs need to be kept at a consistent temperature to incubate properly. Aim for a temperature between 80 and 85°F. The incubation period usually lasts between 45 and 60 days, depending on the temperature and other factors. It's important to monitor the humidity levels to ensure the eggs do not dry out. Keeping the environment stable is crucial for the eggs to develop and hatch successfully.

4. Hatching: As the eggs approach hatching time, you'll see the hatchlings starting to break through the eggshells. Let the hatchlings emerge on their own and avoid helping them unless it's absolutely necessary. They need time to hatch

naturally. Once they have hatched, provide a warm and secure environment for them to thrive.

5. Caring for Hatchlings: After hatching, the baby geckos will need their own enclosure with the right temperature gradients, humidity, and hiding spots. Feed them small insects such as pinhead crickets or small mealworms. Make sure they have access to fresh water at all times. Keep a close eye on their health and development. Regular check-ups will help ensure that they are growing well and adjusting to their new environment.

CHAPTER ELEVEN

SEASONAL CARE ADJUSTMENTS

Seasonal Temperature And Lighting Changes

Leopard geckos come from hot, dry areas and are used to a stable environment. However, they need their habitat adjusted to reflect natural seasonal changes.

Spring and Summer: In the warmer months, your leopard gecko needs a basking spot with a temperature between 88°F and 92°F (31°C - 33°C). This warmth is important for their digestion and health. The cooler side of their enclosure should be kept between 75°F and 80°F (24°C - 27°C). It's essential to use a reliable thermometer to keep track of these temperatures.

Fall and Winter: As temperatures drop, you'll need to adjust the heat source to keep the right temperatures. For the basking area, aim for a range of 85°F to 88°F (29°C - 31°C). The cooler side should be between 70°F and 75°F (21°C - 24°C). You might need a heat mat or ceramic heat emitter to maintain these temperatures. It's crucial to keep a consistent temperature gradient so your gecko can regulate its body temperature effectively.

Lighting: Leopard geckos don't need UVB lighting like some other reptiles, but a proper light cycle is still helpful. Aim for a 12-hour light and 12-hour dark cycle to mimic their natural day-night rhythm. During the warmer months, ensure your gecko gets 12 hours of light and 12 hours of darkness. In the cooler months, you can slightly adjust the lighting schedule, but try to avoid sudden changes. A consistent light cycle helps keep their internal clock regular and supports their overall health.

Preparing For Brumation (Hibernation)

Brumation is a period of reduced activity and metabolic slowdown that some leopard geckos go through in response to cooler temperatures. Not all leopard geckos will brumate, especially if they are kept in warm environments. However, if your gecko does enter brumation, it's important to be prepared.

Recognizing the Signs of Brumation:

If your leopard gecko starts eating less, becomes less active, and spends more time hiding, it might be preparing for brumation. These are natural behaviors as the gecko responds to cooler temperatures and shorter days. ***Preparing the Habitat:*** To prepare your gecko's habitat for brumation, you need to gradually lower the temperature in its enclosure over a few weeks. Start by reducing the basking area temperature to about 80°F (27°C). On the cooler side of the enclosure, aim for a temperature range of 65°F to 70°F (18°C - 21°C). This gradual cooling helps your gecko adjust to the changing conditions.

It's also important to maintain adequate humidity in the habitat. Brumating geckos may not drink as often, so keeping the habitat humid helps prevent dehydration. Regularly check the humidity levels and ensure they are appropriate for your gecko's needs.

Monitoring Your Gecko's Health:
Even during brumation, keep a close eye on your gecko's health. Monitor its hydration levels and watch for any unusual changes in behavior or weight. If your gecko seems sick or loses weight rapidly, it's important to consult a veterinarian.

Ending Brumation: When brumation is over, which may be after a few weeks or months, you need to gradually bring the temperature and lighting back to normal. Slowly increase the temperature in the enclosure to encourage your gecko to become more active. Return the basking area to its usual temperature and adjust the light cycle to a normal day/night routine. This will help your gecko resume regular eating and activity patterns.

Managing Seasonal Behavior Shifts

Leopard geckos are fascinating pets, and their behavior can change with the seasons. Understanding these changes can help you keep your gecko happy and healthy throughout the year.

Spring and Summer: When the weather warms up, you'll likely notice that your leopard gecko becomes more active. They might be on the move more often and have a bigger appetite. To accommodate their increased activity, make sure their habitat is well-suited to their needs. Provide plenty of hiding spots and climbing areas to keep them entertained. Regularly check that they have enough food and fresh water to meet their heightened needs. This is a time when they may need more frequent feedings, so be sure to adjust their diet accordingly.

Fall and Winter: As the temperatures drop, your gecko's behavior will shift. They might become less active and eat less, which is completely normal. This reduced activity level is their way of conserving energy in cooler weather. During these cooler months, you should reduce their food intake. Even though they eat less, it's important to always provide access to fresh water. Keep a close eye on their weight and overall health. If you notice that your gecko is much less active than usual or seems stressed, check their habitat to make sure it's still suitable. If you have concerns about their well-being, consult a veterinarian who can provide guidance and ensure there are no underlying health issues.

CHAPTER TWELVE

CLEANING AND MAINTENANCE

Daily, Weekly, And Monthly Cleaning Tasks

Daily Cleaning Tasks:

1.   Remove Uneaten Food: Every day, check your leopard gecko's enclosure for any leftover food. Remove any uneaten food promptly to prevent it from spoiling and attracting pests, which can lead to health issues for your gecko.

2.   Spot Clean: Daily, look for any waste or soiled bedding. Use a small scoop or spatula to remove feces and dirty substrate. This helps keep the environment clean and reduces odors.

3. Check Humidity and Temperature: Make sure the humidity and temperature in the enclosure are at the right levels for your leopard gecko. Adjust them as needed to ensure your pet remains comfortable and healthy.

Weekly Cleaning Tasks:

1. Replace Substrate: Once a week, change out the substrate in the enclosure. Remove the old substrate and put down fresh material. This helps manage odors and prevents bacteria from building up.

2. Clean the Water Dish: Wash the water dish thoroughly with hot, soapy water each week. Rinse it well and refill it with fresh water. This prevents harmful bacteria from growing and ensures your gecko has clean drinking water.

3.   Wipe Down Surfaces: Use a clean, damp cloth to wipe down the surfaces inside the enclosure, including the walls and any decorations. This removes dust and debris that may have accumulated.

Monthly Cleaning Tasks:

1.   Deep Clean the Enclosure: About once a month, do a complete cleaning of the enclosure. Remove all items such as decorations, hiding spots, and substrate. Wash the enclosure with a reptile-safe disinfectant and rinse it thoroughly to remove any residues.

2.   Inspect and Clean Heating Elements: Check the heating pads, lamps, and other temperature control devices to make sure they are working properly. Clean them according to the manufacturer's

instructions to prevent dust buildup and ensure they function effectively.

3. Replace and Sanitize Hides and Decor: Clean any hides and decorations using a reptile-safe disinfectant. Rinse them well and let them dry completely before putting them back into the enclosure.

Safe Cleaning Products And Methods

When it comes to cleaning your leopard gecko's habitat, it's important to use cleaning products and methods that are safe for your pet. Here are some guidelines to help you keep your gecko's home clean and safe:

1. Use Reptile-Safe Disinfectants: Look for disinfectants made specifically for reptile enclosures. These products are

designed to kill bacteria and fungi without leaving behind harmful residues that could be toxic to your gecko. Avoid using household cleaners as they often contain chemicals that can be dangerous for reptiles.

2. Opt for Natural Cleaners: If you prefer a more natural cleaning method, you can use a mixture of vinegar and water. Vinegar is a safe and effective option for cleaning surfaces in your gecko's habitat. To make this solution, mix one part vinegar with two parts water. Apply the mixture to the surfaces of the enclosure, then rinse everything thoroughly to ensure that no vinegar remains. This method helps eliminate bacteria while being gentle on your gecko.

3.　　Avoid Strong Smells: Cleaners with strong odors can be irritating to your gecko. To maintain a comfortable environment, use mild, unscented cleaning products. Strong-smelling chemicals can cause stress or discomfort for your pet, so it's best to stick with products that are gentle and odor-free.

In addition to choosing the right cleaning products, here are a few more tips to ensure your gecko's habitat stays safe and clean:

A.　　Regular Cleaning: Clean the enclosure regularly to prevent the buildup of waste and bacteria. A clean environment helps keep your gecko healthy and reduces the risk of infections.

B.   Spot Cleaning: Remove any waste or uneaten food daily to keep the habitat clean. This will help reduce odors and maintain a sanitary environment.

C.   Deep Cleaning: Perform a thorough cleaning of the enclosure periodically. This includes washing all surfaces, replacing substrates, and checking for any signs of mold or mildew.

Preventing Parasites And Infections

Keeping your leopard gecko healthy involves preventing parasites and infections, which can be managed by maintaining a clean habitat and monitoring their well-being. Here's how you can ensure your gecko stays in top shape:

1. Regular Cleaning

Maintaining cleanliness is crucial to preventing parasites and infections. Stick to a cleaning schedule that includes daily, weekly, and monthly tasks. Daily, check the enclosure for any waste and remove it promptly. Weekly, clean the water dish and replace the water to keep it fresh. Every month, perform a thorough cleaning of the entire enclosure, including washing all surfaces and accessories with a reptile-safe cleaner. Keeping the habitat clean helps to eliminate bacteria and parasites that could make your gecko sick.

2. Monitor Health

Pay close attention to your gecko's behavior and health. Look for signs that might indicate illness, such as changes in eating habits, unusual behavior, or alterations in their droppings. Healthy leopard geckos are active, eat regularly, and have normal, firm droppings. If you notice anything out of the ordinary, such as lethargy, loss of appetite, or diarrhea, consult a veterinarian who specializes in reptiles. Early detection of health issues can prevent more serious problems down the road.

3. Quarantine New Additions

When introducing new items or animals into the enclosure, it's important to quarantine them first. This means keeping any new additions separate from your existing gecko for a period of time. Quarantine helps to ensure that any potential parasites or diseases do not spread to your gecko's habitat. For new reptiles, keep them in a separate enclosure and monitor them closely for any signs of illness before introducing them to your gecko's living space.

4. Regular Vet Check-ups

Regular visits to a reptile veterinarian are essential for maintaining your gecko's health. Schedule routine check-ups to ensure that any potential health issues are caught early. A reptile vet can provide valuable guidance on how to maintain a healthy environment for your gecko and offer advice on preventing common health problems. They can also help you understand the best practices for keeping your gecko's habitat in top condition.

CHAPTER THIRTEEN

ENRICHMENT AND STIMULATION

Creating A Stimulating Environment

A stimulating environment is key to keeping your leopard gecko happy and healthy. In the wild, these geckos are always on the move, hunting, and finding places to hide. To make your pet's home more like their natural habitat, you should set up an enclosure that encourages these natural behaviors.

First, choose a terrarium that is big enough for your gecko. A larger space provides more room for your pet to explore and helps keep them from getting bored. Inside the terrarium, add a variety of elements to make it interesting. You can use live or fake plants to create visual interest and offer places for your gecko to hide. Hiding spots are essential because they give your gecko a sense of security and a place to retreat when they feel stressed.

It's also important to create different temperature zones within the terrarium. In the wild, leopard geckos experience a range of temperatures, so having both warm and cool areas in their enclosure will help them regulate their body temperature. You can achieve this by using heating pads or lamps to create a warm side and keeping the other side cooler. This setup encourages your gecko to move around and explore different parts of their home.

Another key feature is the substrate, or the material that lines the bottom of the terrarium. Leopard geckos enjoy digging and burrowing, so providing a substrate that allows for these natural behaviors is beneficial. You can use sand or a mixture of sand and soil. However, make sure the substrate is safe for your gecko. Some substrates can cause health issues if ingested, so choose one that is easy to clean and won't harm your pet.

Lastly, consider adding enrichment items like climbing branches, rocks, or hides. These additions mimic the natural environment and offer your gecko opportunities for physical and mental stimulation.

Toys, Hides, And Climbing Structures

To keep your leopard gecko happy and healthy, it's important to provide a variety of items in their enclosure. While leopard geckos are not very active climbers, having a mix of toys, hides, and climbing structures can greatly benefit their well-being. Here's how to set up their habitat to keep them engaged:

Hides: Hides are crucial for leopard geckos because they offer a sense of security and help reduce stress. You should include several hide boxes in different parts of the enclosure. It's best to have hides in both the warm and cool areas of the terrarium. This way, your gecko can choose a hide that matches their temperature preference. You can use ceramic, plastic, or rock hides—whatever you prefer—as long as they are easy for your gecko to enter and exit comfortably.

Toys: While leopard geckos don't play with toys like mammals do, they still benefit from some interactive elements. Simple items such as a small mirror can spark curiosity and provide visual stimulation. However, be cautious with toys—avoid anything with small parts that could be swallowed. The goal is to provide something that catches their attention and encourages exploration without posing a risk.

Climbing Structures: Although leopard geckos are not natural climbers, adding a few climbing structures can make their habitat more interesting. Consider including low branches or rocks that your gecko can use to perch or explore. These structures should be stable and securely placed to ensure your gecko's safety. The aim is not to make the enclosure a climbing playground, but rather to offer a variety of levels to encourage a bit of exploration.

Digging Materials: Leopard geckos love to dig, so providing suitable materials for burrowing is essential. Use reptile sand or a soil mix to create a digging area. This activity helps keep your gecko mentally stimulated and satisfied. Make sure the digging materials are clean and free from any harmful substances.

Mental And Physical Enrichment Activities

To ensure your leopard gecko stays mentally and physically stimulated, it's important to add variety to their routine. Here are some easy and effective ways to keep your gecko engaged and healthy:

1.   Food Puzzles: Make mealtime more interesting by hiding your gecko's food in

different spots around their enclosure. You can place insects under logs or in small containers to encourage your gecko to hunt and forage. You could also use special feeding dishes that make them work a little for their food. This helps to activate their natural hunting instincts and keeps them mentally sharp.

2. Varied Diet: Feeding your leopard gecko a range of different insects can also be stimulating. While crickets and mealworms are common, introducing other types of insects can add variety. You might also try gut-loading the insects with different nutrients before feeding them to your gecko. Changing up their diet now and then can make feeding time more exciting and provide additional mental enrichment.

3. Exploration Time: Allowing your gecko to explore outside their enclosure, under your watchful eye, can offer them new sensory experiences. Set up a safe, secure play area with various textures and objects for them to explore. This not only keeps them physically active but also exposes them to new smells and sights, making their environment more stimulating.

4. Interactive Sessions: Spend time gently handling your gecko and introducing them to new experiences. It's important that these interactions are calm and stress-free, as too much handling or sudden changes can be harmful. Regular, gentle interaction can help your gecko become more comfortable with you and their environment.

5. Temperature Variations: Adjusting the temperature gradients in their enclosure from time to time can mimic natural environmental changes. By providing a range of temperatures, you encourage your gecko to move around more and explore different parts of their habitat. This variation can also help keep their metabolism active and mimic their natural habitat conditions.

CHAPTER FOURTEEN

TRAVELING WITH YOUR GECKO

Safe Transport Methods

When transporting your gecko, choosing the right container is crucial for its safety and comfort. Here's a simple guide to help you prepare for the journey:

Choosing the Right Container

Select a container that is secure, well-ventilated, and the right size for your gecko. A small, sturdy plastic or glass terrarium with secure latches is ideal. These containers prevent escapes and keep your gecko safe. If the trip is short, a small travel carrier with ventilation holes can also work. The container needs to be well-ventilated to ensure your gecko gets enough air and doesn't overheat or suffocate.

Preparing the Container

Line the bottom of the container with paper towels or soft cloths. These materials are easy to clean and will absorb any accidents that might occur during travel. Avoid using loose bedding like sand or wood chips, as these can be ingested or cause respiratory problems for your gecko.

Making Your Gecko Comfortable

To help keep your gecko calm during the trip, add familiar items to the container. Place a small hide box or a piece of its usual substrate inside. These familiar items provide a sense of security and can reduce stress. Your gecko will feel more comfortable if it recognizes the smells and objects from its home environment.

Handling the Container

Keep the container steady during transport to avoid jostling. Sudden movements or rough handling can stress your gecko, so be gentle and try to keep the container as stable as possible. If you're driving, place the container on a flat surface in the car to prevent it from moving around.

Traveling Long Distances

Traveling long distances with your gecko requires careful planning to ensure their safety and comfort. Whether you're driving, flying, or taking a train, it's important to address your gecko's specific needs.

If you're driving, make sure to take regular breaks to check on your gecko. The temperature inside the car can change quickly, becoming too hot or too cold. Use a portable fan or heater to keep the temperature stable and comfortable. Avoid leaving your gecko in a car alone, as the temperature can become extreme very fast. During breaks, ensure your gecko's container is secure and that they have access to water. Only let them out of their container if absolutely necessary.

For longer journeys, such as flights or train rides, you'll need to follow specific guidelines for traveling with reptiles. Most airlines and train services have regulations for transporting animals, including requirements for a health certificate from a veterinarian. Make sure to check these regulations well before your trip to ensure you meet all the requirements.

Before a long flight, it's best to avoid feeding your gecko to prevent nausea or digestive problems. If you must make a stop, offer water to keep them hydrated, but try to avoid taking them out of their container unless it's crucial. Having a travel plan that includes all necessary health and emergency information for your gecko will help you stay prepared in case of any issues.

Settling Your Gecko After Travel

After traveling, the first thing you need to do is help your gecko settle into its new environment. Start by placing its enclosure in a quiet, calm area. This will help your gecko adjust slowly and comfortably. If the journey was long, give your gecko a few days of peace and limit handling to allow it to recover from the stress of travel.

Keep a close eye on your gecko for any signs of stress or health issues. Look out for changes in appetite, unusual lethargy, or different behavior from what you usually see. It's normal for your gecko to take a few days to get back to its usual routine, so be patient and attentive during this time.

Reintroduce your gecko to its regular feeding schedule slowly. Start by offering small amounts of food and observe how it responds. Always provide fresh water in its enclosure. This is crucial for your gecko's hydration and overall health.

Make sure the habitat conditions in the enclosure are just right. Check the temperature and humidity levels to ensure they meet your gecko's specific needs. Consistent and proper habitat conditions help your gecko feel secure and make the transition smoother.

CHAPTER FIFTEEN

LEOPARD GECKO BEHAVIOR

Understanding Normal Vs. Abnormal Behavior

Leopard geckos are popular reptiles known for their easygoing nature and relatively low-maintenance care. They exhibit a range of behaviors that are completely normal, which helps ensure they are happy and healthy in their environment.

Normal Behavior: Leopard geckos are nocturnal, which means they are most active during the evening and night. You might see them exploring their habitat, hunting for insects, or basking under a heat lamp. These activities are perfectly normal and part of their natural behavior. Leopard geckos also shed their skin periodically. This shedding is a sign of healthy growth and should occur regularly. Another common behavior is the use of their tails for balance. They might wave their tails or use them to signal distress if they feel threatened. These actions are typical and show that the gecko is functioning normally.

Abnormal Behavior: It's important to watch for any changes in behavior that might indicate a problem. If your leopard gecko becomes excessively lethargic, refuses to eat, or displays unexpected aggression, these could be signs of stress or illness. For example, a gecko that hides all the time or moves its tail in unusual ways might be experiencing discomfort. Repetitive pacing, where the gecko walks back and forth in a confined space, is another abnormal behavior that can suggest health issues or stress.

Observing these behaviors closely helps in understanding the health of your gecko. If you notice any of these unusual behaviors, it's important to investigate further or consult a veterinarian who specializes in reptiles. Regular check-ups and a proper habitat setup can help prevent many of these issues.

Common Behavioral Problems And Solutions

1. Loss of Appetite: If your leopard gecko suddenly stops eating, it can be a sign of a problem. This might be due to stress, incorrect habitat conditions, or health issues like parasites. To address this, first check that the temperature and humidity in the gecko's habitat are correct.

Make sure they have a variety of food available and watch for any signs of illness. If your gecko continues to refuse food, it's a good idea to consult a veterinarian who specializes in reptiles to find out what might be wrong.

2.   Aggression: Although leopard geckos are usually gentle, they can sometimes act aggressively. This might include biting or whipping their tail, especially if they feel threatened. Aggression can occur due to improper handling, territorial disputes, or discomfort from their environment. To reduce aggression, handle your gecko gently and less often during stressful periods. Ensure their enclosure is spacious and comfortable. When introducing new geckos, do so gradually to prevent conflicts over territory.

3. Excessive Hiding: Leopard geckos will naturally hide from time to time, but if your gecko is hiding all the time, it could be a sign of stress, incorrect temperature, or illness. Make sure their habitat has proper hiding spots and that the temperature is right. If your gecko is consistently avoiding the outside world and not eating, it might be sick. In such cases, a visit to the vet is recommended.

4. Tail Waving: Leopard geckos use tail waving as a way to communicate. This behavior is often seen when they are excited or exploring their environment. However, if your gecko's tail waving becomes excessive or is accompanied by signs of distress, it could be a sign of stress or health issues. Pay attention to other

behaviors and consult a vet if you're concerned.

5. Digging or Burrowing: Digging or burrowing is a natural behavior for leopard geckos. They may do this as part of their normal activities. But if you notice that this behavior becomes obsessive or is linked with other signs of distress, it might indicate a problem with their habitat or health. Check the setup of their enclosure to ensure it meets their needs and watch for other signs that might indicate an issue.

Interpreting Gecko Body Language

Being able to interpret your leopard gecko's body language can help you better understand its feelings and health. Here are some key signs to watch for:

1.   Tail Movement: The tail is a major indicator of your gecko's emotions. If you notice your gecko's tail wagging quickly, it could mean they are excited or feeling aggressive. A tail held high often shows that the gecko is curious or alert. On the other hand, if the tail is drooping, it might be a sign of fear or discomfort.

2.   Body Posture: How your gecko holds its body can reveal a lot about how it feels. When a gecko stands upright with a straight body, it's usually a sign that it is alert and interested in its surroundings. If your gecko hunches down or flattens itself against the ground, it might be feeling threatened or stressed. This kind of posture can indicate that the gecko is trying to make itself less noticeable or is simply not comfortable.

3. Hissing or Vocalizations: Leopard geckos are not very noisy, but they might make sounds like hissing when they are scared or upset. If you hear your gecko making these noises, it's a good idea to check if something is bothering them. These vocalizations are their way of communicating discomfort or agitation.

4. Shedding Behavior: Leopard geckos shed their skin regularly as they grow. If you see your gecko rubbing against surfaces or soaking in water, it is likely getting ready to shed. This behavior is normal and part of their natural growth process. It's important to provide a proper environment for shedding, such as a moist hide or soaking dish, to help them shed smoothly.

5. Eating Habits: How much and how often your gecko eats can be a good indicator of its health. A healthy leopard gecko will usually have a good appetite and eat regularly. If you notice a decrease in their appetite or they are not eating as much as usual, it could be a sign of health issues or stress.

☐

CHAPTER SIXTEEN

LEOPARD GECKO MYTHS AND MISCONCEPTIONS

Debunking Common Myths

Leopard geckos are fascinating pets, but there are several myths about their care that can lead to confusion. Let's clear up some common misconceptions:

1. Leopard Geckos Need Complete Darkness

A widespread myth is that leopard geckos are strictly nocturnal and must be kept in total darkness. While it's true that leopard geckos are more active at night, they don't need their habitat to be pitch black. Instead, they thrive on a day/night light cycle that simulates natural conditions. A low-intensity light during the day helps regulate their internal clock and keeps them healthy.

2. Leopard Geckos Don't Need Heat

Another misconception is that leopard geckos can live comfortably at room temperature without any additional heat. In reality, leopard geckos are ectothermic, meaning they rely on external heat to maintain their body temperature. Without a proper heat source, such as a heat mat or heating lamp, they can develop health problems and have trouble digesting their food. Providing a temperature gradient in their enclosure allows them to choose a comfortable spot.

3. Leopard Geckos Eat Only Insects

Some people think that insects are the only food leopard geckos need. While insects should be a major part of their diet, they also need a variety of foods to stay healthy. A balanced diet for leopard geckos includes different types of insects, and it's important to offer gut-loaded and calcium-dusted prey. Occasionally, specialized gecko food can also be beneficial to ensure they get all the necessary nutrients.

4. Leopard Geckos Don't Need Supplements

It's a common myth that leopard geckos don't need any supplements if they eat a varied diet. However, leopard geckos do need calcium and vitamin supplements to prevent deficiencies. Calcium powder should be sprinkled on their food regularly, and a multivitamin supplement can be given from time to time to cover all their nutritional needs.

5. Leopard Geckos Can Be Housed Together

Some believe that leopard geckos can live together without any issues. In fact, leopard geckos are solitary animals and can become territorial. Housing them together can lead to stress, fights, and injuries. It's best to keep leopard geckos individually to ensure they remain healthy and stress-free.

Understanding Leopard Gecko Facts

Leopard geckos are fascinating reptiles native to the dry, rocky regions of Asia and the Middle East. These areas are characterized by their arid climate, which is why leopard geckos have evolved to thrive in such environments. In the wild, they are solitary creatures, spending their days hidden in crevices or burrows to stay cool and safe from predators. At night, they emerge to hunt for insects, which make up their primary diet.

One of the standout features of leopard geckos is their long lifespan. With proper care, these geckos can live between 15 to 20 years, making them a long-term commitment for pet owners. They grow at a slow and steady pace, reaching their full size within about 18 to 24 months. Understanding their growth patterns is important for providing the right habitat and diet as they mature.

Leopard geckos go through a regular shedding process as they grow. This shedding of their skin is a natural and essential part of their development. To help them shed comfortably and avoid problems like stuck shed, it's important to provide a humid hide. This moist environment aids in the shedding process, making it easier for the gecko to remove its old skin.

In terms of communication, leopard geckos have their own unique ways of expressing themselves. They use a combination of vocalizations and body language to interact with each other. For example, they might produce clicks or chirps to communicate. By paying attention to these sounds and observing their body movements, you can gain insight into their needs and emotional states. Understanding these forms of communication can help you provide better care and respond more effectively to your gecko's needs.

☐

CHAPTER SEVENTEEN

ADVANCED CARE TIPS

Transitioning From Beginner To Advanced Care

Moving from basic to advanced care for your gecko involves refining their living space, understanding their complex needs, and adopting advanced care techniques. Here's how you can enhance their environment and well-being:

1. Upgrade the Enclosure: If you're ready to advance, consider upgrading your gecko's enclosure. A larger or more specialized habitat can better mimic their natural environment. Ensure the enclosure includes proper temperature gradients, humidity levels, and suitable substrates. Investing in high-quality lighting and heating elements, like UVB lights and heat

mats, will help maintain optimal conditions for your gecko.

2. Fine-Tune Temperature and Humidity: Leopard geckos need a controlled temperature to thrive. Purchase precise thermostats and hygrometers to accurately monitor and adjust the temperature and humidity in their habitat. Create a thermal gradient within the enclosure, offering a range of temperatures so your gecko can move between warmer and cooler areas to regulate their body temperature effectively.

3. Enhance Enrichment and Stimulation: To keep your gecko engaged and happy, add enrichment elements to their enclosure. Include various hides, climbing structures, and substrates that allow for burrowing and exploring. Regularly rearrange or introduce new items to

provide mental and physical stimulation, preventing boredom and encouraging natural behaviors.

4. Monitor Health Closely: Keep a close eye on your gecko's health by observing their behavior, appetite, and physical appearance. Look out for any changes or signs of health issues. Regular check-ups and being attentive to their needs will help you catch potential problems early and address them promptly.

Exploring Advanced Gecko Health And Nutrition

Taking care of a gecko goes beyond just feeding them. To ensure your gecko stays healthy and happy, it's important to understand their diet and be vigilant about any health issues they might face. Here's a simple guide to advanced gecko care:

Diet and Nutrition: While a basic diet often includes gut-loaded crickets or mealworms, advanced care means offering a more varied menu. Provide a range of insects like dubia roaches, black soldier fly larvae, and waxworms. This helps ensure your gecko gets a balanced intake of nutrients. Don't forget to add calcium and vitamin D3 supplements to prevent deficiencies and promote overall health.

Feeding Schedule: Your gecko's feeding schedule should be adjusted according to their age, size, and activity level. Younger geckos usually need to eat more often, while adults can be fed less frequently. Regularly check your gecko's weight and adjust their diet to avoid issues like obesity or malnutrition.

Hydration: Always provide fresh water for your gecko. Use a shallow dish and change the water regularly to keep it clean. In addition to water, consider misting their habitat occasionally or providing a moist hide to help with hydration.

Health Issues: Watch out for common health problems such as metabolic bone disease (MBD), impaction, and skin infections. Regularly check your gecko for any signs of illness. If you notice anything unusual, such as changes in behavior or appearance, consult a reptile vet right away. Being familiar with signs of stress or illness will help you provide timely care.

Record Keeping: Keep a health journal for your gecko. Record their feeding schedule, shedding times, and any health issues. This journal will help you track their health over time and provide useful information to your veterinarian if needed.

Expanding Your Gecko Collection

Expanding your gecko collection can be an exciting venture, but it's important to approach it with care to ensure the health and happiness of all your geckos. Here's a straightforward guide to help you make this process smooth and successful.

1. Do Your Research: Before you bring new geckos into your home, spend time learning about their specific needs. Different species and morphs (varieties) of geckos have unique care requirements and temperaments. For example, some geckos might need special diets, specific temperatures, or unique habitat conditions. Knowing these details will help

you provide the best care for each new addition and ensure they get along well with your current geckos.

2. Quarantine New Geckos: To prevent any potential spread of diseases or parasites, it's crucial to quarantine new geckos before introducing them to your main collection. Set up a separate enclosure for the new geckos and monitor them closely for any signs of illness or parasites. This quarantine period allows you to ensure they are healthy and reduces the risk of passing any issues to your existing geckos. A typical quarantine period is around 30 days, but it can vary depending on the health of the new geckos and your specific situation.

3. Provide Adequate Space: Make sure you have enough space for each gecko.

Overcrowding can cause stress, health problems, and aggression among geckos. Plan your enclosures so that each gecko has enough room to move around comfortably. Each gecko should have its own space to retreat and feel safe. Properly sized enclosures and sufficient hiding spots are essential for maintaining a healthy and stress-free environment.

4. Understand Social Dynamics: Different gecko species have different social needs. While leopard geckos are generally solitary and may not require social interaction, other species might tolerate or even benefit from the company of other geckos. Observe how your geckos interact with each other. If you notice any signs of aggression or stress, be ready to separate them to prevent any harm. Understanding and managing

the social dynamics within your gecko collection is key to maintaining harmony.

☐

THE END